BE A MAKER!

Maker Projects for Kids Who Love

EXPLORING THE OUTDOORS

SARAH LEVETE

Crabtree Publishing Company
www.crabtreebooks.com

Crabtree Publishing Company

www.crabtreebooks.com

Author: Sarah Levete

Series Research and Development: Reagan Miller

Editors: Sarah Eason, Harriet McGregor,
Tim Cooke, and Philip Gebhardt

Proofreaders: Claudia Martin, Wendy Scavuzzo,
and Petrice Custance

Editorial director: Kathy Middleton

Design: Paul Myerscough

Cover design: Paul Myerscough

Photo research: Rachel Blount

**Production coordinator and
Prepress technician:** Tammy McGarr

Print coordinator: Katherine Berti

Consultant: Jennifer Turliuk, Bachelor of Commerce,
Singularity University Graduate Studies Program at
NASA Ames, Former President of MakerKids

Production coordinated by Calcium Creative

Photo Credits:

t=Top, bl=Bottom Left, br=Bottom Right

Ellie Irons: www.ellieirons.com: p. 15; Shutterstock: Bikeriderlondon:
p. 10–11; ChameleonsEye: p. 27; Olesia Bilkei: p. 4; File404: p. 10;
FreeProd33: p. 14; Mandy Godbehear: p. 6; Robert Adrian Hillman: pp. 1,
26; Holbox: p. 22; Littleny: p. 25; Nico99: p. 16; Oliveromg: p. 5; Peresanz:
p. 19; PhotoSerg: p. 24; Pixelparticle: p. 18; Praisaeng: p. 17; Paul Reeves
Photography: p. 23; Aigars Reinholds: p. 9; Studio0411: p. 8; Waldru: p. 7;
Tudor Photography: pp. 12–13, 20–21, 28–29.

Cover: Tudor Photography

Library and Archives Canada Cataloguing in Publication

Levete, Sarah, author
    Maker projects for kids who love exploring the outdoors
/ Sarah Levete.

(Be a maker!)
Includes index.
Issued in print and electronic formats.
ISBN 978-0-7787-2576-3 (hardback).--
ISBN 978-0-7787-2582-4 (paperback).--
ISBN 978-1-4271-1764-9 (html)

    1. Nature craft--Juvenile literature. 2. Handicraft--Juvenile
literature. I. Title.

TT160.L447 2016   j745.5   C2016-903329-5
                                         C2016-903330-9

Library of Congress Cataloging-in-Publication Data

Names: Levete, Sarah, author.
Title: Maker projects for kids who love exploring the outdoors /
Sarah Levete.
Description: St. Catharines, Ontario ; New York, New York :
Crabtree Publishing Company, [2016] | Series: Be a maker! |
Includes index.
Identifiers: LCCN 2016026030 (print) | LCCN 2016026734 (ebook)
ISBN 9780778725763 (reinforced library binding) |
ISBN 9780778725824 (pbk.) |
ISBN 9781427117649 (Electronic HTML)
Subjects: LCSH: Nature craft--Juvenile literature. | Natural
history projects--Juvenile literature. | Handicraft--Juvenile
literature. | Makerspaces--Juvenile literature.
Classification: LCC QH55 .L48 2016 (print) | LCC QH55 (ebook)
| DDC 745.5--dc23
LC record available at https://lccn.loc.gov/2016026030

Crabtree Publishing Company

www.crabtreebooks.com   1-800-387-7650

Printed in Canada/072016/EF20160630

Published in Canada
Crabtree Publishing
616 Welland Ave.
St. Catharines, Ontario
L2M 5V6

Published in the United States
Crabtree Publishing
PMB 59051
350 Fifth Avenue, 59th Floor
New York, New York 10118

Published in the United Kingdom
Crabtree Publishing
Maritime House
Basin Road North, Hove
BN41 1WR

Published in Australia
Crabtree Publishing
3 Charles Street
Coburg North
VIC, 3058

CONTENTS

EXPLORE AND MAKE!

If you like adventure, activity, being outside, teaming up with friends, and making the most of your world, then read on. The outdoors is nature's free learning and fun zone. There are endless opportunities to try new skills, develop confidence with problem-solving, and simply enjoy the natural world. If you want to stretch all your skills, from math to creativity, get out there and enjoy the natural world around you!

MAKER MOVEMENT

The maker movement is about learning through hands-on experience. Get your hands dirty, discover new things, be inspired to create and make with the natural materials outside your front door. Team up with your friends to make the most of your adventures and exploration. It is a perfect way to share ideas and find solutions to difficulties and challenges.

Use this book to guide you in outdoor exploration. Use it to inspire you. There are three projects in the book—but they are just suggestions. When you are working on a project or have completed one, discuss with your friends ways it could be improved or changed. Being a maker is about trying new activities, learning from them, and being willing to adapt or improve things.

From early morning adventures to moonlit camps, there is always something to do and experience outdoors.

MAKERSPACES

The maker movement is all about sharing ideas with others so that your projects and activities are **collaborative**. Making the most of the outdoors and exploration is part of the maker movement. A place where people can gather to share **resources** and knowledge, and work on projects is called a **makerspace**.

SAFETY

Follow these basic rules to ensure you keep yourself and your friends safe when you are exploring:

- Always tell a responsible adult where you are going and when you are expected home.
- Stay together as a group.
- Wash your hands before eating.
- Watch out for insects and bugs that bite.
- Never touch or eat plants unless you know it is safe to do so.
- If you are going on a long hike, take basic first-aid supplies such as adhesive bandages and ointment for insect bites.
- Take water to drink.

ATTITUDE

The most important part of adventure and exploration is mental attitude. In any challenging situation, you need to think clearly and remain positive. Work as a team to get the best from each person. **Perseverance** is the key—do not give up!

Explore the amazing outdoor world with your friends and share opportunities to create maker projects together.

THE GREAT OUTDOORS

Explore outdoors anywhere in the world—or anywhere outside your front door! The outdoors is there to discover. Investigate fields, forests, woodlands, hills, mountains, rain forests, ponds, rivers, the seashore, and, yes, even backyards. You do not need to go far to explore!

RESPECT NATURE

Show respect for the natural **environment**. Nature is the greatest **recycler**. Little is left to waste. Use this to inspire your projects and leave nothing to waste yourself. Challenge yourself and your friends to use only those materials or objects that you find in their natural state, or that you can reuse. Follow these guidelines so your exploration does not upset the natural balance of the environment, but works alongside it:

- Avoid deliberately disturbing natural **habitats**. If you pick up a bug, carefully replace it where you found it.
- Take home any trash. Leave only your footprints.
- Only use branches and twigs that have naturally broken or fallen.
- Do not pick wildflowers or plants, as this can affect their survival.

Take care not to harm any creatures you find—remember, the outdoors is their home.

Be a Maker!

Arrange to go hiking with a group of friends. Leave behind all technology (although one person can keep a cell phone for emergency contact, if required). Before you go, ask parents and older relatives about the outdoor games and activities they played when they were young. As a group, choose some of these traditional games and activities to try. Think about the differences between these games and the games you usually share with your friends. Discuss with your friends if there are ways to combine some of the traditional outdoor activities with the technological games and resources you are used to.

Use your imagination to come up with games for which you need only twigs, leaves, and a maker spirit.

MAKING THE MOST OF MOTHER NATURE

Enjoying the outdoors brings huge physical and emotional benefits. It is a fun and foolproof way to keep fit. Walk, cycle, or jog your way in the outdoors. Fresh air helps you breathe in more **oxygen**, which you need to survive. If you are stressed by schoolwork or just want some time away from your usual routine, nature is a great remedy. Marvel at the mysteries of the world. Take a deep breath and quietly observe. Enjoy the sounds, smells, sights, and feel of the amazing natural world around you.

DISCOVERY

The maker movement encourages people to **reinvent**, or change, what already exists. The outdoors is perfect for such an imaginative approach. Whenever you and your friends try any of the activities suggested in this book, or other activities you think of, look at everything around you with fresh eyes. Exploration and discovery can take place in even the most familiar areas.

BE PREPARED

Take responsibility as a group to ensure everyone's safety and well-being. This will help keep you safe and allow you to make the most of the outdoors. Include these items in your backpack:

Compass: invaluable if you are using a map
Map: essential if you are venturing far or going on a new route
Water bottle: important in the hotter months
Sun protection: important in the summer months
Food: you need an energy-boosting snack if you are out for a long time
Cell phone and notepad: for emergencies and to take notes of any interesting finds

Leave behind any mapping app on your cell phone. Use a compass and your map-reading skills to guide you. They do not need batteries!

GEOCACHING

Geocaching brings together technology and nature. It is an outdoor treasure-hunt that uses a **Global Positioning System (GPS)** to find "treasure" based on **coordinates**. The treasure is hidden in places known as "caches." These can be anywhere. The treasure may be puzzles to be solved, messages left by others, or small toys. Once you have found the treasure, sign the log.

Design your own treasure hunt in two teams. One team designs a treasure trail using technology to provide the clues. Another uses traditional clues. Test them both. Pool your ideas about making improvements and decide how you can involve others in your **community** in this outdoor activity.

If you try geocaching, make sure you follow coordinates from an established geocaching website. Always tell a responsible adult where you are going.

Geocache treasure can be puzzles, clues, small gifts, or anything to encourage others to share the fun of the hunt.

Makers and Shakers

Tim Eggleston

Tim Eggleston, from West Virginia, loved the excitement of finding a geocache and opening it. It inspired him to design his own caches that look like birdhouses, but with a puzzling twist! Searchers have to find a way to unlock a birdhouse that is built like a puzzle. Lots of people wanted to know how Tim built them, so he decided to share his passion on YouTube so that others can build and invent their own geocaches.

BUG BONANZA

Wherever you go outdoors, look closely and you will spot crawling beetles, flying insects, and weaving spiders. These creepy crawlies are some of the most extraordinary creatures. Each one is **adapted** to its habitat. Bugs provide endless opportunities for people to marvel at their physical make-up and be wowed by their incredible skills.

WAIT AND WATCH

To find out more about the tiny creatures beneath your feet and flying above your head, you need to be observant, patient, and ready to record your observations. Take a magnifying glass with you so you can take a close-up look. Take photos, so you can carry out more detailed research into the type of bug you are looking at. Look for the tiny critters under leaves or logs, crawling over rocks, or chilling in pools and ponds. If you want a closer look, carefully place a glass jar over the bug and then slip a piece of cardboard across the opening. Note the time, the place, the weather, and what the bug was doing. Release the bug after you have examined it.

Record observations on a cell phone or notepad, so you can compare and contrast what happens on different hikes.

SPIDER WATCH

About 900,000 **species** of insects and spiders have been **identified** and given names, but many more have yet to be discovered. In 2014, 12-year-old Australian Robert Beeton was working with a group to find and name new species of spiders. At the end of a long, hot day, the group was tired and ready to go home. Except for Robert who continued to lift up pieces of bark and peer under logs. Robert's perseverance paid off. He discovered a new species of spider, which he named Paruwi.

With a watchful eye, an open mind, and perseverance, you never know what you will discover. Share your observations with your maker friends.

Be a Maker!

Use your understanding and knowledge of insects and bugs to create puzzles and games for others to enjoy when exploring outdoors. With a friend, make a large-scale model of an insect or bug from recycled cardboard. Cut it into large jigsaw-sized pieces. Hide these in a park or similar place. Challenge others to find the pieces and identify the insect and its features. What other ways can you think of to combine further understanding of the natural world with an enjoyable game?

MAKE IT!
BUG HOUSE

Make a bug house to attract insects. You can use only recycled materials. This is a great activity to share with friends. Discuss with your friends what kinds of materials are most attractive to a range of bugs.

YOU WILL NEED
- Old **pallet** with supports
- Garden canes
- Pine cones
- Straw
- Drainpipe
- Broken plantpots
- Garden hose
- Cardboard

1
- Search for natural and recycled materials.
- Plan your design based on your materials.

2
- Cut your pallet into three sections. Stack the sections on top of each other in the site you choose for your bug house. Make sure the structure is secure and does not wobble.
- Ask an adult to cut material, such as canes, to size.

3

● Discuss with your friends where to place the bug house. Then fill each section of your bug house with different materials. There is no need to use glue, but you could secure small pieces with net or chicken wire. This also adds extra protection against hungry birds.

● Try to pack each section fairly tightly with material. Try combining materials with different **textures**. If there are large gaps, add extra wood or other natural material. Rotting wood is ideal for beetles and spiders.

4

CONCLUSION

How does the completed bug house compare with your plans? Did everything you planned turn out to be possible to achieve? Look at the different sections of the bug house and discuss with your friends which parts you think will attract most bugs and why.

Make It Even Better!

Look at the bug house and reflect on how you could improve it. Is it in the best location to attract bugs? Discuss with your friends if there are other natural materials you can usefully add to the house. How can you use this activity to encourage others to understand the importance of tiny creatures in our world?

PLANT POWER

From wild weeds to blossoming blooms, plants and trees shape the landscape. As well as being a source of food, plants help provide essential oxygen. Plants are home to an endless number of insects and other creatures. And they are the basis for many of the medicines we rely on.

PLANT PROTECTION

Most plants are harmless, but some—even common plants—are deadly. The poison in some plants protects them from being eaten by animals. Oleander, a pretty plant that grows in some gardens, contains a poison that can kill. Even the smoke from burning oleander is dangerous. The manchineel tree, which is native to Florida, Central America, the Caribbean, and northern South America, may be the world's most poisonous tree. It is painted with a warning red cross to keep people from touching it. Never eat a plant growing wild, unless you are sure it is not toxic (poisonous). Always wash your hands after handling any plants.

If you cannot safely identify a plant, do not touch it—and definitely do not eat it.

Makers and Shakers

Ellie Irons

Do you stop to notice the weeds and plants that grow near sidewalks? U.S. artist Ellie Irons (born 1981) does! She creates dyes from weeds and uses them to paint—she has even picked weeds from the grounds of a maker faire, where people interested in the maker movement go to share ideas. Ellie combines her interest in biology and the natural world with her passion as an artist. Can you think how to create paint from a plant or flower? What else can you make from a sweet-smelling bud? Experiment and share with your friends. Remember, the process is as important as the product you create.

Flowers are colorful and scented. What could you create from them?

AWESOME ADAPTERS

Choose several different species of plant. Observe them and note how they have adapted to their environment. Consider any threats to their survival. List the uses and benefits of these plants. With your friends, gather some recycled objects and natural materials from a forest or park. Use these to design and create a new plant. Think about what you want the plant to provide and how you want it to look. Does your design improve on nature's product?

NATURAL INVENTION

Makers take inspiration from the world around them. Team up with some friends to investigate different plants and animals. Note their physical characteristics or features, and how they adapt to their habitat. What can you learn from the natural world and then apply to solve an everyday problem? Share ideas with your friends. Be open to everyone's ideas and use each idea to help inspire another.

LOOK AND OBSERVE

A branch of science called **biomimicry** draws on the incredible design and **function** of animals and plants to find solutions to everyday problems for humans. But to observe and understand creatures, we have to find ways of reaching them. It is easy to explore what is within reach, but it is more challenging to explore higher up or underground. Explorers and scientists have to come up with practical and smart ways to do this.

The gecko's sticky toes have inspired inventors and scientists. Observe other creatures to see what we can learn from them and consider how we can use this knowledge.

Makers and Shakers

George de Mestral

The Swiss engineer George de Mestral (1907–1990) began his career as a maker at age 12, when he designed a toy airplane. Many years later, in 1948, George was out hiking with his dog. When he arrived home, he saw that **burrs** were sticking to his clothes and the dog's fur. He took a microscope to look closely at a burr. He discovered it was covered with tiny hooks that caught on materials such as clothing and fur. After more than eight years of work, George created what is known today as Velcro.

Without George de Mestral's curious maker spirit, we may not have the sticky Velcro we use so much today.

Climbing trees, traveling in hot-air balloons, constructing walkways between the tree-tops, and digging deep underground—these are some of the ways to study the world above and below us. Can you think of other ways?

STICKY IDEAS

Have you ever wondered how a gecko runs up a wall or hangs from a ceiling? For centuries, scientists have been amazed by this ability. In 2003, researchers at the University of Manchester created an artificial version of a gecko's sticky feet. Gecko tape has a similar structure to a gecko's toe pad. It is made from a different material, but it is created following the same principles.

NIGHT AND DAY

Nature never sleeps. Camp out with your friends to experience the wonder of the natural world by day and night. You do not need to camp in the woods or a forest. Your backyard will do. Go for a flashlight walk or walk by moonlight. What insects and animals can you see and hear that are not around during the day?

ASTRONOMICAL AWE

Take a blanket and a flashlight outside on a clear night. Let your eyes adjust to the darkness. What you can spot in the dark sky? There may be a **galaxy**, a shooting star, or a planet. Can you see the Milky Way? Earth is part of the Milky Way. It is a spiral galaxy that is more than 100,000 **light years** in diameter with at least 100 billion stars! Look for it when the moon is not out, and when you are far away from the **artificial** lights of towns or cities that light up the night sky.

Wrap up warmly and gaze in wonder at a starry sky.

MAKE THE MILKY WAY

Make your own Milky Way to help you understand its structure. Take an old compact disk (CD) or cut a circle of black bristol board. Glue some cotton balls to either side of the CD or bristol board. Pile them up in the middle, with fewer toward the edges. This represents the galaxy's center, often called a bulge. The CD or bristol board represents the disk that contains stars, gas, and dust. After looking at the Milky Way and researching its structure, what other features can you add to your model?

Before you go out, do some research, so you know what you are looking at!

Be a Maker!

Early sailors used the rising and setting stars to help them **navigate**, or find their way. Research and identify the key **constellations** (patterns of stars) you need to navigate. But first, figure out if you are facing north or south without using a compass. For this, use your research to identify the constellation known as the **Big Dipper** or the **Plow**. Draw an imaginary line joining the two stars at the end of the Big Dipper, then extend that line by five times its length "up" into the sky. The line will reach a star that seems brighter than the others. This is **Polaris**, or the **North Star**. In the Northern Hemisphere, it always indicates north. What advantages and disadvantages might this form of navigation have?

MAKE IT!
SUNDIAL

You can create your own way of telling the time, using the sun! Find out how by making your own sundial.

YOU WILL NEED
- Paper plates
- Drinking straw
- Pen and ruler
- Duct tape
- Scissors
- Push pins or knitting needle
- Watch or cell phone

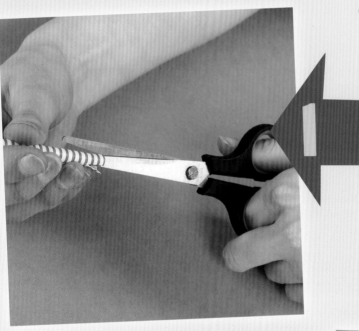

1

- Find the center of a paper plate. First fold a plate in half, then in half again. Unfold it and lay it on top of a new plate. Stick a pin through the center of the creased cross to mark the center of the other plate.
- Cut four snips upward into the end of the straw (left).

- Widen the hole until you can push the end of the straw through the unfolded plate. On the underside of the plate, bend and flatten the straw pieces outward. Tape them to the plate.
- Draw a line from the straw to the edge of the plate. Write the number 12 at the top.

2

3

- Place the plate in the sun and secure in place with push pins, or by sticking a knitting needle down through the straw into the ground. It will be easiest to read your sundial if you go outside at noon and line up the straw's shadow on the plate at the 12 mark.
- Note every hour during the afternoon on your watch or cell phone, then mark where the shadow of the straw falls.

4

- Start again in the morning, until you are back at 12.

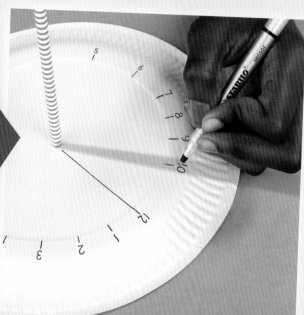

Make It Even Better!

How reliable do you think this sundial is? Where would you choose to position it outside to work most effectively? If you worked as a group, share your thoughts with your teammates.

CONCLUSION

Now test your sundial. Make observations about how effective it is. What other ways could you use the power of the sun?

RUN WILD

Some of the most exciting books and beautiful paintings are inspired by the great outdoors. When you are outdoors, let your imagination run wild. The wilderness or even your own backyard can fire up your imagination and creativity.

MAKE A STORY

Gather some friends around a campfire, or even on a blanket in your backyard. Take turns to tell a story, make up a poem, or sing a song inspired by the great outdoors. Collect some stories from your parents and relatives. Write them in a special book. Challenge yourself to create a book from entirely natural or recycled materials. Experiment with writing on leaves, or making your own paper—this is best done with friends. Bind the book with dried bark that has fallen from trees. Is the "paper" you have used suitable for writing, or do you need to find a different way of writing on it?

Think of themes for stories, and encourage each other to share them. Think of ways that you can develop your stories.

WORKING WITH NATURE

An artist or creator does not always need years of experience, a studio, and special equipment. Take a fresh look at the objects around you. A stone or pebble has a **unique** shape. No two twigs are exactly alike. Create a sculpture or picture using found items. How long will your creation last before weather and time take their toll?

EXPECT THE UNEXPECTED

Sometimes, it will be cloudy when you want a clear sky. In some locations, there might be too much noise and activity to see wild creatures. Rethink your plans! Being a maker is about finding solutions to problems.

Take off your headphones and take time to listen to the world around you. What do you hear?

Be a Maker!

Insects and bugs are noisy creatures. Stop to listen to their calls and sounds. Listen to birds. With your friends, go outdoors with some recording equipment or a cell phone that will record sounds. Listen carefully for insect sounds and walk quietly toward them. Can you find the insect making the sound? Can you watch it to see how the sound is made? What else can you learn from the sounds you hear?

PROTECT!

The outdoors is one of our most precious resources. Yet it is under constant threat from humans. We contribute to **climate change** and the destruction of forests. It is up to everyone to make the time to help protect our natural environment.

TAKE RESPONSIBILITY

Everyone can contribute to protecting our planet from the effects of **pollution** and gases that lead to climate change. The maker movement is determined to help preserve natural resources. Team up with some classmates to design posters. Perhaps focus on the relationship between energy use and the release of harmful **greenhouse gases**. These gases trap heat in the atmosphere and contribute to the climate change that threatens our planet.

Make an amazing sculpture out of recycled material. This plastic-bottle elephant could be used to help make people aware of problems caused by our use of plastic.

RECYCLE

In the United States alone, about 4 million plastic bottles are used every hour. Only 25 percent of them are recycled. What happens to the remaining 75 percent? Lots of them end up in **landfill** sites. Garbage buried in landfill sites takes up a huge amount of space. All sorts of wild animals live in landfill sites, which is harmful for them and is not their natural habitat. What we do every day can have an impact on the outdoors and the creatures that live there.

Bring the community together to improve your outdoor spaces.

Be a Maker!

Did you know that more than 80 percent of plants rely on honeybees and other pollinators to reproduce? However, pollinators are in decline. Work your maker magic with some friends to do your bit for these critters. You can do this in a patch in your backyard or in a window box, but why not see if there is an unused area in your community where you can create a pollinator patch? (Make sure you have permission to use the site.) Encourage native pollinators such as butterflies and beetles by growing native plants (research them on the Internet or at your library). Make a plan of what you will grow and encourage everyone to join in this maker project that can have a lasting effect.

SKILLS IN THE WILD

If you and your friends want to test your outdoor skills, which skills do you think would be most important—and why? Put these three requirements—fire, water, and shelter—in order of importance. Share your list with friends and see if they agree.

FIRE IT UP

A fire provides warmth for your body and heat to cook. It provides light and can be used to attract attention if you are stranded. It wards off biting insects, too! The best way to light a fire is by using a magnifying glass. You can focus the sun's rays on **tinder**, such as dry grass, dry leaves, or wood shavings. Small fires require less fuel than large fires, so keep the fire small. Only build the fire in a safe place (a clearing)—not near flammable trees or brush. Only make a fire when there is a responsible adult present.

DRINK

You can survive for days if necessary without food, but you can only survive three days without water. A clean supply of water is essential for survival. Boiling water on your fire will get rid of most germs, but you need a container to boil it in. How could you purify, or kill bacteria in, water? Are there any plants that store water—and how safe is it to drink from them?

Fire is useful for cooking, keeping warm, and boiling water to make sure it is safe.

TAKE SHELTER

When building a shelter, consider the location. Is it far enough away from hazards such as insect nests or falling branches? Is it near enough to the building materials you will need to use? A shelter needs to be large enough for you to lie down in. Think about the best structure. A flat roof may collapse under heavy rain, for example.

A shelter needs to withstand wind and rain. It needs to be strong enough so it does not collapse on top of you.

Be a Maker!

Knots can fix tricky problems! You can use cord from a parachute, called paracord, which is strong and can be used for many different purposes. Or challenge yourself and your friends to come up with a way to create your own cord. Look at the reeds and grasses around you for inspiration. There are many different ways to tie a knot. Try the figure eight, which is a basic strong knot. Why are there so many different types of knots? Are there any new and more effective ways that you can figure out to tie a knot?

MAKE IT!
BUILD A SHELTER

You will need to work as a team to carry out this activity. You will also need to think logically and practically, as well as creatively.

1

- Take 10 garden stakes and tape them together in pairs, 12 inches (30 cm) from the top and bottom.
- Arrange three of the double stakes in a pyramid, so they cross about 10 inches (25 cm) from the top. Tie them together with string. Add the other two double stakes, so there are two at the front and three at the back.

2

- Join three tarps together down their long edges with duct tape. The middle section should be overlapped by the first and third sections for extra protection.
- Standing at the front, wrap the tarp around the stakes like a jacket. It should be tight at the top.

- Secure the top with some rope or tape. Some tarps have eyelets around the bottom, so tent pegs can be hammered into the ground to secure the shelter.

3

4

- Wrap camouflage netting around the top for added detail. Secure in place with string, rope, or tape.
- Put your ground sheet or mat inside for somewhere to sit.

CONCLUSION

Once your shelter is up, discuss with your team what you felt worked well and what could have been done differently. How did it feel to work collaboratively on this maker project? Could you have accomplished it by yourself?

Make It Even Better!

Try out your shelter. What conditions do you need it to withstand? As a team, discuss how you could improve the shelter if you had different materials.

GLOSSARY

adapted Changed to suit conditions

artificial Made by humans

biomimicry A branch of science that copies characteristics of animals and plants to use in everyday life

burrs Spiky balls covered in hooks that are old seed heads of plants

climate change The global change in Earth's weather

collaborative Sharing ideas

community People around you who you can join in with

constellations Groups of stars that form recognizable patterns

coordinates Numbers used to indicate a position on a map

environment The natural world around you

function Purpose

galaxy A system of millions or billions of stars, gas, and dust

geocaching A treasure hunt in which clues or puzzles are hidden at spots indicated by GPS coordinates

Global Positioning System (GPS) A satellite-based navigation system made up of a network of satellites

greenhouse gases Gases that cause Earth's atmosphere to heat up

habitats Places where animals and plants live

identified Established what something is

landfill Waste material that is disposed of by burying it in the ground

light years Units of distance based on how far light travels in one year

makerspace A place where makers come together to share ideas

navigate To find your way

oxygen A gas in the air that humans and animals need to live

pallet A movable wooden platform on which goods are stacked

perseverance Determination

pollinators Insects, birds, or animals that carry pollen to help plants reproduce

pollution Substances released into nature that damage it

recycler Someone who reuses something, often for a purpose other than the one it was designed for

reinvent Think of new ways of doing something

resources Things we use; materials

species Groups of similar organisms

textures The feel of different surfaces

tinder Small bits of dry leaves or grass used to start a fire

unique Unlike any other

LEARNING MORE

BOOKS

Colson, Rob. *Ultimate Survival Guide for Kids*. Firefly Books, 2015.

Editors of TIME For Kids Magazine. *Time For Kids Book of How: All About Survival*. TIME for Kids, 2014.

Howard, Melanie A. *Camping For Kids* (Into the Great Outdoors). Capstone Press, 2012.

Miles, Justin. *Ultimate Explorer Guide for Kids*. Firefly Books, 2015.

WEBSITES

Check out this website for some cool tips and challenges for camping:
https://diy.org/skills/camper

If you want to challenge your tracking powers, take a look:
https://diy.org/skills/tracker

Here are great tips on hiking for young trekkers:
www.americanhiking.org/kids

This website provides lots of useful links to outdoors projects:
www.makezine.com

INDEX